PACIFIC CO
TREE FINDER

a pocket manual for identifying Pacific Coast trees

by Tom Watts

To identify a tree:

- Select some typical leaves or needles and turn to page 6.

- Make the first choice, either or and go on from there.

- After a few more choices you'll come to a drawing and the name of your tree.

Advice: See pages 1 - 5 before you begin.

Note: **This book is for trees that grow naturally in this area.** ▶

It does not identify introduced trees except for a few widely-planted species which have become somewhat naturalized in the area.

Maps in this book show the natural ranges of trees.

Symbols show the place within its range where you're likely to find each tree growing:

 **— on warm, sunny ridges —** These trees grow slowly with roots in dry, rocky soil, where wind blows away the snow and shapes their resinous foliage. Among them you'll find lairs and lizards.

 ← on streambanks or in soggy soil — These trees grow fast, have shiny, pliable foliage, easily broken twigs, soft wood, and birds.

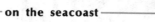 **← on the seacoast ——** These are often trees which grow only on windy slopes facing the sea, usually in sandy soil.

 ← in burned areas — Unless fire returns, these trees will eventually be replaced by more shade-tolerant species.

 ← in abandoned farmyards, old settlements These trees grow so well on the Pacific coast they may seem to be native species, but they or their ancestors were planted here.

other symbols: (more on pages 2 - 5)

 deciduous trees These are leafless in winter or the dry season.

 shrubby trees These are trees that often grow as shrubs and become trees only on sheltered slopes and canyons.

The climate of this area has damp, foggy sea air, a long growing season, and abundant rain. It supports a deep, dark, ferny forest where trees must compete for sunlight.

This is the symbol for the **dominant trees** of this forest.

They grow rapidly, straight upward toward the light. Before clearcut logging the shade kills back lower trunk branches and produces fine-grained, knot-free lumber.

This is the symbol for smaller **understory trees.**

They are shade-tolerant throughout life, and often capture weak light with thin, broad, horizontally held leaves. They may grow sideways toward a patch of sunlight.

Average Rainfall (inches per year)

over 128 in.

64 to 128

32 to 64

16 to 32

8 to 16

under 8 in.

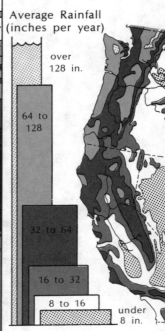

The Pacific coast climate is dryer toward the south and in the low-altitude inland valleys:

This is the symbol for trees of the **mixed-evergreen forest** of the coast ranges. No big redwoods or hemlocks here. Small Douglas-firs dominate. Leaves here are often thick, leathery, and evergreen. This slows evaporation of moisture during dry summers and takes advantage of mild, wet winters.

This symbol is for trees of the **California oakwoods** where short, muscular-looking, deep-rooted trees with small, bristly leaves stand far apart, or else cluster along canyons and north-facing slopes. Even the pines here look stunted.

Much of this area is a mosaic of woods, grassland, and chaparral (stiff, dry, evergreen shrubbery) on hot slopes.

Acorns from California oaks were a staple food for Indians. They still support woodpeckers.

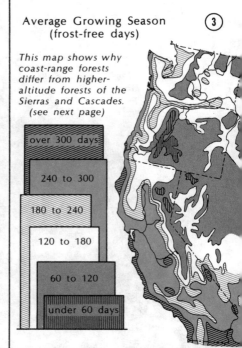

Average Growing Season (frost-free days) ③

This map shows why coast-range forests differ from higher-altitude forests of the Sierras and Cascades. (see next page)

over 300 days

240 to 300

180 to 240

120 to 180

60 to 120

under 60 days

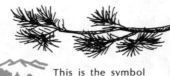

CASCADES

SIERRAS

Climbing into high mountains is like going north (and going north is like climbing). The climate turns colder and usually wetter; and the vegetation resembles the fir forest of Canada. Further up you see small, spire-shaped trees as in interior Alaska. Go high enough and it's treeless like the Arctic barrens.

alpine zone (treeless)

subalpine zone

red fir forest

silver fir forest

mixed conifer forest

Douglas-fir cedar hemlock forest

oak woodland

This is the symbol for trees of the **mixed conifer forest.** The dry lower elevations of this forest are often open pine woods (with chaparral). In higher elevations, more rainfall supports more kinds of trees, larger and closer together.

Most adult trees here have thick, corky trunk bark and can survive small ground fires. Accumulations of unburned undergrowth and fallen wood may support larger, killing fires. Hillside trees may be fire-hollowed on the uphill side where logs roll against trunks and later burn.

 This symbol is for trees of the **mountain fir forest** where branches are shaped to shed heavy snowfall. You'll find curved lower trunks on trees that grew from saplings bent by a thick, sagging snowpack.

Fires are rare here, but wreak disaster when they come to the "tinder-box" of twiggy deadwood and lower branches.

The dense fir forest is on the better soils. Pines grow where it's rockier, and in burned areas. Lodgepole pine grows in mountain basins or "flats" where cold night air drainage collects.

 This symbol is for trees of the **subalpine zone.** To survive here trees must mature their new growth in a short, unreliable summer where you can make snowballs in July and expect frost in late August.

The higher you go, the smaller the trees. Near the upper limit of this zone, trees can survive only where snowdrift seals out the abrasive wind.

 This symbol is for trees likely to grow on the dry **eastern slopes** of high mountains. These are Rocky Mountain trees, adapted to a severe, cold-dry climate.

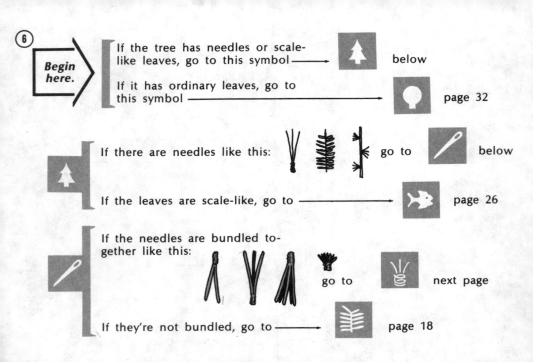

(6)

Begin here.

If the tree has needles or scale-like leaves, go to this symbol → 🌲 below

If it has ordinary leaves, go to this symbol → 💡 page 32

🌲
If there are needles like this: ⋮ 🌿 🌿 go to 🪡 below

If the leaves are scale-like, go to → 🐟 page 26

🪡
If the needles are bundled together like this: ╱ ╱ ╱ 🌾 go to 🔥 next page

If they're not bundled, go to → 🌿 page 18

If the bundles have fewer than six needles, it's a **PINE.** Go to

 next page

If they have more than six, it's a **LARCH.** Go to

below

If the needles are three-sided, it is

WESTERN LARCH
Larix occidentalis

If they're four-sided, it is

SUBALPINE LARCH
Larix lyallii

If the needles are . . .
. . . five to a bundle, go to 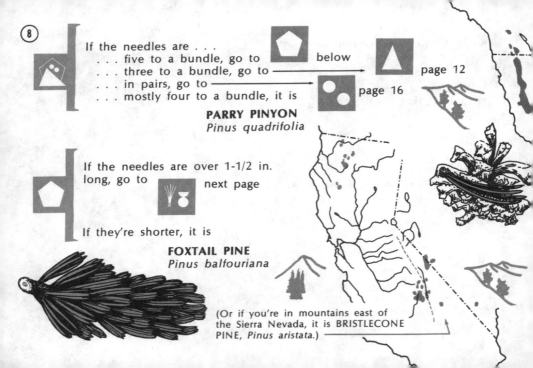 below
. . . three to a bundle, go to ——→ page 12
. . . in pairs, go to ——→ page 16
. . . mostly four to a bundle, it is

PARRY PINYON
Pinus quadrifolia

If the needles are over 1-1/2 in.
long, go to next page

If they're shorter, it is

FOXTAIL PINE
Pinus balfouriana

(Or if you're in mountains east of
the Sierra Nevada, it is BRISTLECONE
PINE, *Pinus aristata*.)

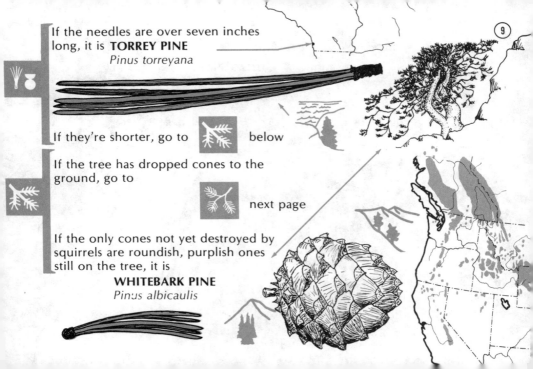

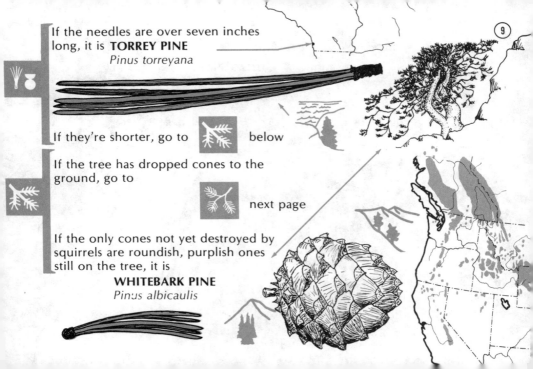

If the needles are over seven inches long, it is **TORREY PINE**
Pinus torreyana

If they're shorter, go to 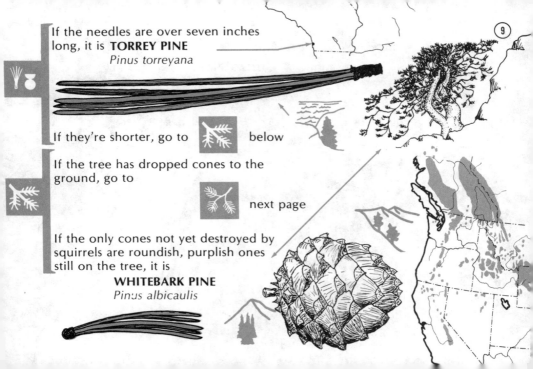 below

If the tree has dropped cones to the ground, go to

 next page

If the only cones not yet destroyed by squirrels are roundish, purplish ones still on the tree, it is

WHITEBARK PINE
Pinus albicaulis

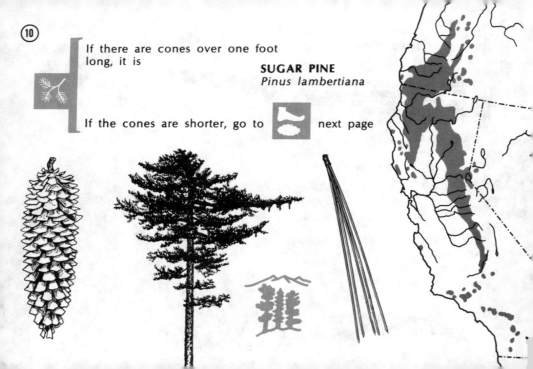

If there are cones over one foot long, it is

SUGAR PINE
Pinus lambertiana

If the cones are shorter, go to next page

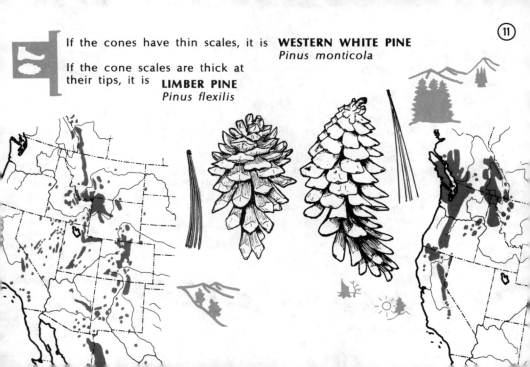

If the cones have thin scales, it is **WESTERN WHITE PINE**
Pinus monticola

If the cone scales are thick at their tips, it is **LIMBER PINE**
Pinus flexilis

If the outermost twigs are thicker than an ordinary wooden pencil (5/16 in.), go to ⟶ below

If they're thinner, go to page 14

If there are long, upward-curved lower branches with blackish bark, or foot-long needles, or dangerous-looking 9 to 14 inch cones, it is **COULTER PINE BIGCONE PINE** *Pinus coulteri*

If the bark is lighter, the needles shorter, and the cones non-violent, go to next page

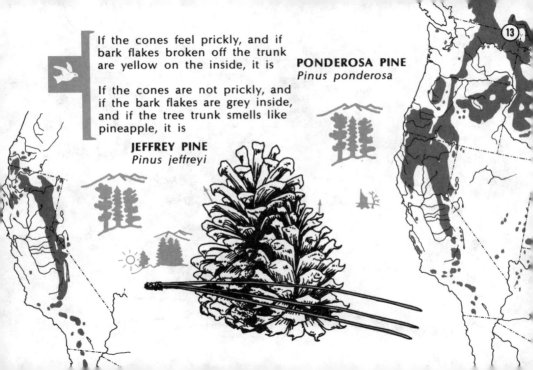

If the cones feel prickly, and if bark flakes broken off the trunk are yellow on the inside, it is

PONDEROSA PINE
Pinus ponderosa

If the cones are not prickly, and if the bark flakes are grey inside, and if the tree trunk smells like pineapple, it is

JEFFREY PINE
Pinus jeffreyi

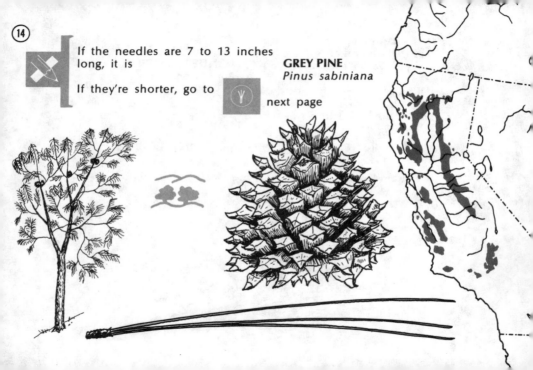

If the needles are 7 to 13 inches long, it is

GREY PINE
Pinus sabiniana

If they're shorter, go to next page

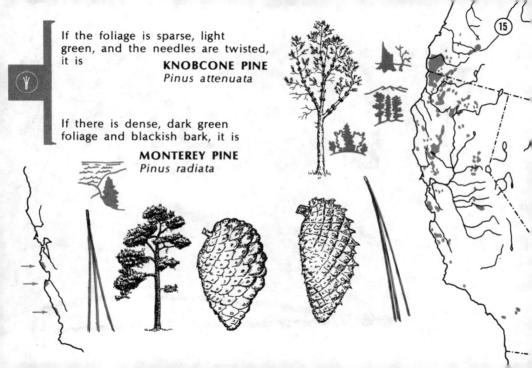

If the foliage is sparse, light green, and the needles are twisted, it is

KNOBCONE PINE
Pinus attenuata

If there is dense, dark green foliage and blackish bark, it is

MONTEREY PINE
Pinus radiata

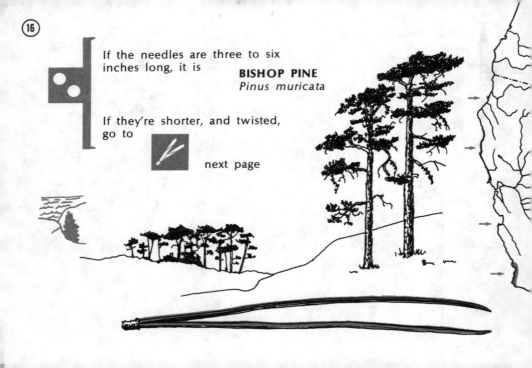

If the needles are three to six inches long, it is

BISHOP PINE
Pinus muricata

If they're shorter, and twisted, go to

next page

If the tree is small or shrubby, and it grows near sea level, it is
SHORE PINE
BEACH PINE
Pinus contorta var. *contorta*

If the tree is larger, or if it grows inland above 3,000 ft. elevation, it is **LODGEPOLE PINE**
TAMRAC PINE
Pinus contorta var. *murrayana*

Cones and needles of these two pines look alike.

In the Cascades north of the Columbia River, you'll find Rocky Mountain Lodgepole Pine (*Pinus contorta* var. *latifolia*).

In the acid, hardpan soils near Mendocino, California, you'll find a pygmy variety called Bolander Pine (*Pinus contorta* var. *bolanderi*).

If there are smooth, round scars where old needles have fallen off the twig, it's a **FIR**. Go to below

Firs also have resin-filled bark blisters and cones that fall apart on the tree instead of dropping to the ground.

If it's not a fir, go to page 22

 If the needles narrow to a stalk where they join the twig, go to below

If they're wide at the base, go to page 21

 If the needle tips are sharp spines, it is **SANTA LUCIA FIR BRISTLECONE FIR** *Abies bracteata*

If not, go to next page

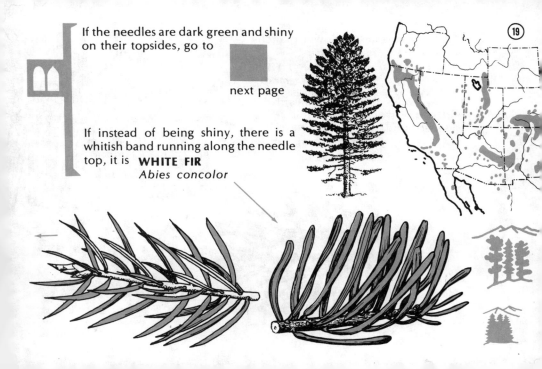

B

If the needles are dark green and shiny on their topsides, go to

next page

If instead of being shiny, there is a whitish band running along the needle top, it is **WHITE FIR**
Abies concolor

(19)

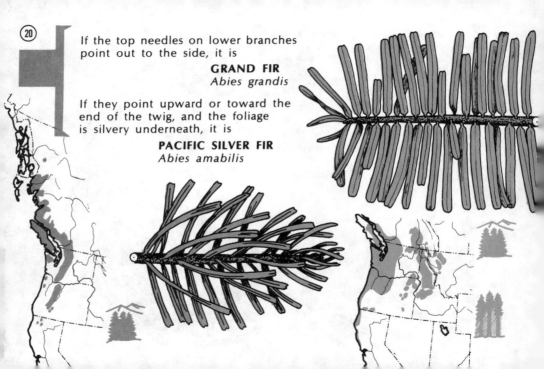

If the top needles on lower branches point out to the side, it is

GRAND FIR
Abies grandis

If they point upward or toward the end of the twig, and the foliage is silvery underneath, it is

PACIFIC SILVER FIR
Abies amabilis

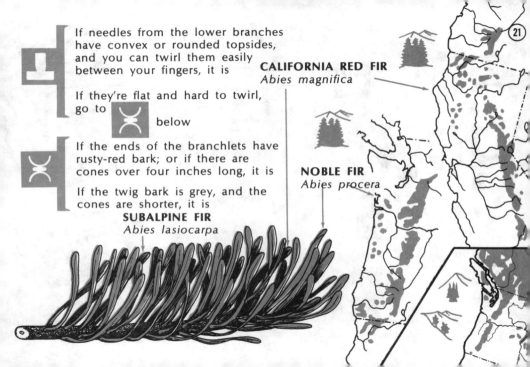

If needles from the lower branches have convex or rounded topsides, and you can twirl them easily between your fingers, it is **CALIFORNIA RED FIR** *Abies magnifica*

If they're flat and hard to twirl, go to [X] below

If the ends of the branchlets have rusty-red bark; or if there are cones over four inches long, it is **NOBLE FIR** *Abies procera*

If the twig bark is grey, and the cones are shorter, it is **SUBALPINE FIR** *Abies lasiocarpa*

If the older twigs from which needles have fallen have stubby pegs on them like this: it's a **SPRUCE.**

Go to  next page

If the twigs are smoother, go to below

If you can easily twirl a needle between thumb and finger, go to below

If the needles are too flat to twirl, go to page 24

If the needles are longer than one inch, it is **SINGLELEAF PINYON**
Pinus monophylla

If they're shorter, it is
MOUNTAIN HEMLOCK
Tsuga mertensiana

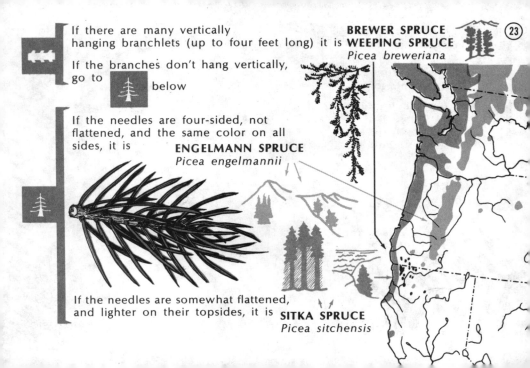

If there are many vertically hanging branchlets (up to four feet long) it is **BREWER SPRUCE WEEPING SPRUCE** *Picea breweriana*

If the branches don't hang vertically, go to below

If the needles are four-sided, not flattened, and the same color on all sides, it is **ENGELMANN SPRUCE** *Picea engelmannii*

If the needles are somewhat flattened, and lighter on their topsides, it is **SITKA SPRUCE** *Picea sitchensis*

23

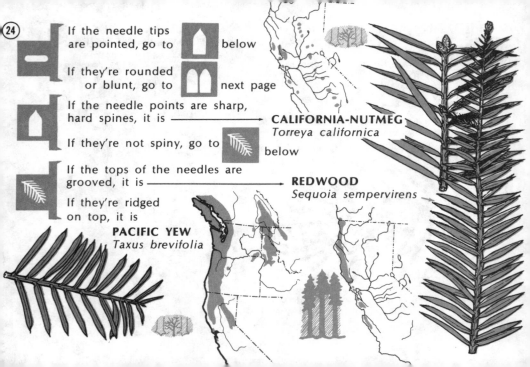

(24)

If the needle tips are pointed, go to ⬒ below

If they're rounded or blunt, go to ⬓⬓ next page

If the needle points are sharp, hard spines, it is ⟶ **CALIFORNIA-NUTMEG**
Torreya californica

If they're not spiny, go to 🌿 below

If the tops of the needles are grooved, it is ⟶ **REDWOOD**
Sequoia sempervirens

If they're ridged on top, it is

PACIFIC YEW
Taxus brevifolia

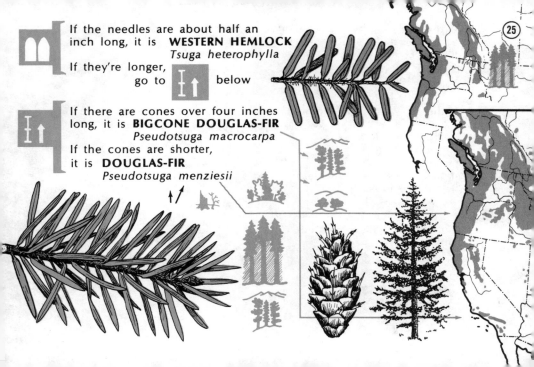

If the needles are about half an inch long, it is **WESTERN HEMLOCK** *Tsuga heterophylla*

If they're longer, go to below

If there are cones over four inches long, it is **BIGCONE DOUGLAS-FIR** *Pseudotsuga macrocarpa*

If the cones are shorter, it is **DOUGLAS-FIR** *Pseudotsuga menziesii*

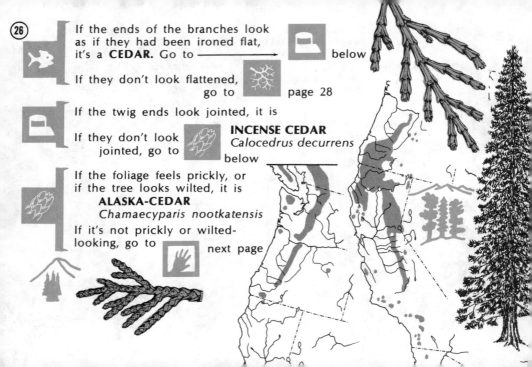

If the ends of the branches look as if they had been ironed flat, it's a **CEDAR.** Go to ⟶ below

If they don't look flattened, go to page 28

If the twig ends look jointed, it is

If they don't look jointed, go to below

INCENSE CEDAR
Calocedrus decurrens

If the foliage feels prickly, or if the tree looks wilted, it is
ALASKA-CEDAR
Chamaecyparis nootkatensis

If it's not prickly or wilted-looking, go to next page

If the foliage is glossy and very fragrant, or if there are leathery, oblong cones, it is

WESTERN RED-CEDAR
Thuja plicata

If you can rub a whitish bloom off the foliage, and there are round cones, it is

PORT-ORFORD-CEDAR
Chamaecyparis lawsoniana

If there are awl-shaped leaves arranged spirally on the twig, it is **GIANT SEQUOIA**
Sequoiadendron giganteum

If the leaves are in opposite pairs instead of a spiral, go to **➤◄** below

If there are roundish, woody, cone-like fruits 1/2 inch or more in diameter, it's a **CYPRESS.** Go to next page

If there are smaller, juicy or pulpy, berry-like fruits, it's a **JUNIPER.** Go to page 30

If you can't find fruit, you may have a male tree. Find a female.

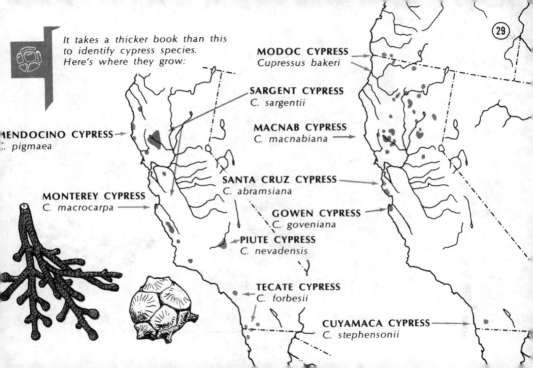

It takes a thicker book than this to identify cypress species. Here's where they grow:

MODOC CYPRESS
Cupressus bakeri

SARGENT CYPRESS
C. sargentii

MACNAB CYPRESS
C. macnabiana

MENDOCINO CYPRESS
C. pigmaea

SANTA CRUZ CYPRESS
C. abramsiana

MONTEREY CYPRESS
C. macrocarpa

GOWEN CYPRESS
C. goveniana

PIUTE CYPRESS
C. nevadensis

TECATE CYPRESS
C. forbesii

CUYAMACA CYPRESS
C. stephensonii

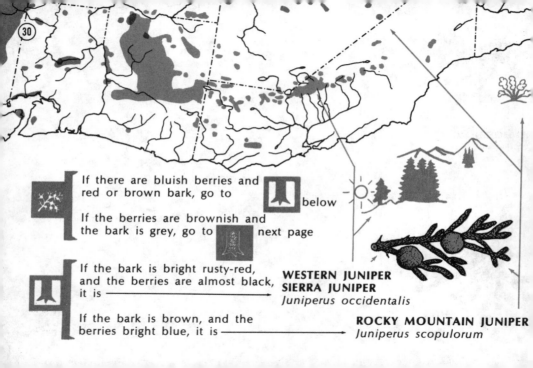

If there are bluish berries and red or brown bark, go to ▯ below

If the berries are brownish and the bark is grey, go to ▮ next page

If the bark is bright rusty-red, and the berries are almost black, it is ⟶ **WESTERN JUNIPER SIERRA JUNIPER** *Juniperus occidentalis*

If the bark is brown, and the berries bright blue, it is ⟶ **ROCKY MOUNTAIN JUNIPER** *Juniperus scopulorum*

If you're west of the Sierra Nevada, or if the leaves are conspicuously dented, it is **CALIFORNIA JUNIPER** *Juniperus californica*

If you're east of the Sierras, or if the leaves are not conspicuously dented, it is **UTAH JUNIPER** *Juniperus osteosperma*

(32)

If the leaves are compound, composed of three or more leaflets, like this:

There's a bud on the twig at the base of a leaf, but not at the base of a leaflet.

go to 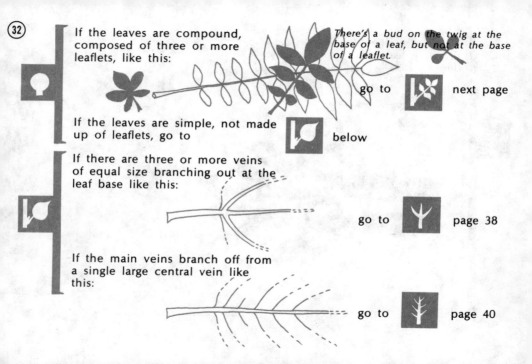 next page

If the leaves are simple, not made up of leaflets, go to below

If there are three or more veins of equal size branching out at the leaf base like this:

go to page 38

If the main veins branch off from a single large central vein like this:

go to page 40

If the leaves have eight of more leaflets, go to  below

If there are fewer leaflets, go to  page 35

If the leaflet margins are saw-toothed, it's a **WALNUT.** Go to  next page

If they're not saw-toothed, go to  below

If there are rounded leaflets and thorns, it is **BLACK LOCUST**
Robinia pseudoacacia

If not, go to  below

If the leaves smell bad, it is **AILANTHUS**
Ailanthus altissima

If they smell spicy, it is **CALIFORNIA PEPPER TREE**
Schinus molle

from China

from Peru

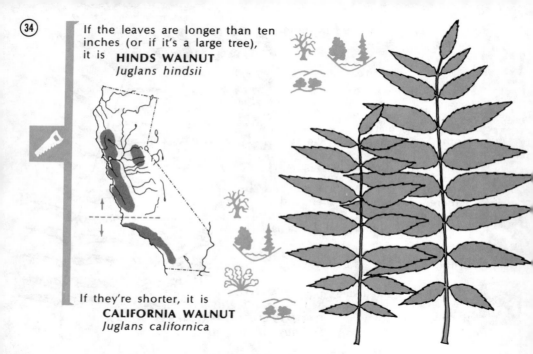

(34)

If the leaves are longer than ten inches (or if it's a large tree), it is **HINDS WALNUT** *Juglans hindsii*

If they're shorter, it is **CALIFORNIA WALNUT** *Juglans californica*

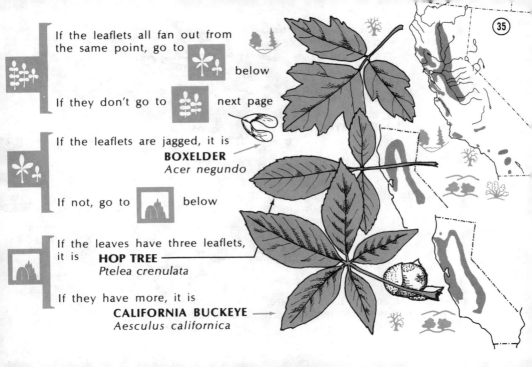

If the leaflets all fan out from the same point, go to

below

If they don't go to

next page

If the leaflets are jagged, it is
BOXELDER
Acer negundo

If not, go to

below

If the leaves have three leaflets, it is **HOP TREE**
Ptelea crenulata

If they have more, it is

CALIFORNIA BUCKEYE
Aesculus californica

If the leaflets have saw-toothed margins, and tips tapered like this:

. . . or if there are small berries, it's an **ELDERBERRY**. Go to below

If not, it's an **ASH**. Go to next page

If the teeth on the margin run all the way to the tip of the leaflet; or if berries are red, or flower clusters are dome-shaped, it is

PACIFIC RED ELDER
Sambucus callicarpa

If the tip of the leaflet is without teeth; or if berries are blue, or flower clusters flat, it is **BLUE ELDERBERRY**
Sambucus caerulea

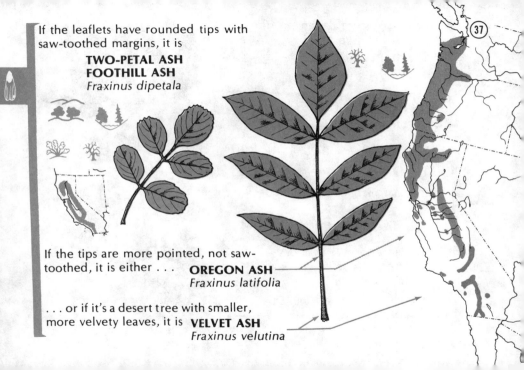

If the leaflets have rounded tips with saw-toothed margins, it is

TWO-PETAL ASH
FOOTHILL ASH
Fraxinus dipetala

If the tips are more pointed, not saw-toothed, it is either . . . **OREGON ASH**
Fraxinus latifolia

. . . or if it's a desert tree with smaller, more velvety leaves, it is **VELVET ASH**
Fraxinus velutina

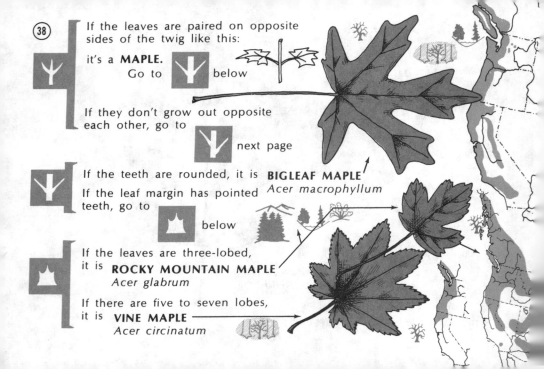

(38) If the leaves are paired on opposite sides of the twig like this:

it's a **MAPLE**.
Go to ⟨symbol⟩ below

If they don't grow out opposite each other, go to ⟨symbol⟩ next page

If the teeth are rounded, it is **BIGLEAF MAPLE**
Acer macrophyllum

If the leaf margin has pointed teeth, go to ⟨symbol⟩ below

If the leaves are three-lobed, it is **ROCKY MOUNTAIN MAPLE**
Acer glabrum

If there are five to seven lobes, it is **VINE MAPLE**
Acer circinatum

If the leaves are lobed go to below

If they're not lobed, go to below

If the leaves are almost round, it is **CALIFORNIA REDBUD**
Cercis occidentalis

If they're narrower (or if you see blue flowers), it is
BLUEBLOSSOM
Ceanothus thyrsiflorus

If the leaves are over four inches wide, it is **CALIFORNIA SYCAMORE ALISO**
Platanus racemosa

If they're smaller, and fuzzy, it is **FLANNELBUSH**
Fremontodendron californicum

(40)

If the leaf is lobed like this: it's an **OAK.**
Go to below

If it's not lobed, go to page 42

If the lobes are pointed, go to below

If they're rounded, go to next page

If the lobes are shallow, it is

ORACLE OAK
Quercus X morehus

If they're deeper; or if the leaves are over four inches long, it is

CALIFORNIA BLACK OAK
Quercus kelloggii

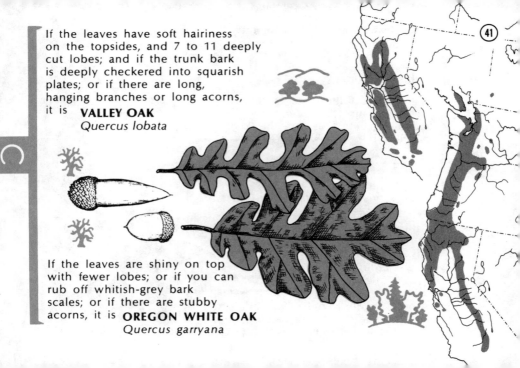

If the leaves have soft hairiness on the topsides, and 7 to 11 deeply cut lobes; and if the trunk bark is deeply checkered into squarish plates; or if there are long, hanging branches or long acorns, it is **VALLEY OAK**
Quercus lobata

If the leaves are shiny on top with fewer lobes; or if you can rub off whitish-grey bark scales; or if there are stubby acorns, it is **OREGON WHITE OAK**
Quercus garryana

If the leaf stems are over an inch long, go to ———→ below

If they're shorter, go to page 44

If the leaves flutter in a gentle breeze because their stems are flattened where they join the leaf like this ———→

go to next page

If the stems are not flattened that way, go to ———→ below

If there are sticky twigs and rounded teeth on the leaf margin, it is **BLACK COTTONWOOD**
Populus trichocarpa

If there are shiny red twigs and sharp, outward-pointing teeth along the leaf margin, it is OREGON CRAB APPLE (see p. 56)

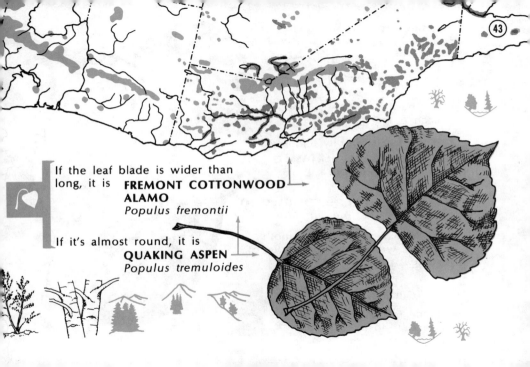

If the leaf blade is wider than long, it is **FREMONT COTTONWOOD ALAMO**
Populus fremontii

If it's almost round, it is **QUAKING ASPEN**
Populus tremuloides

If the leaves grow in pairs opposite each other on the twig like this:

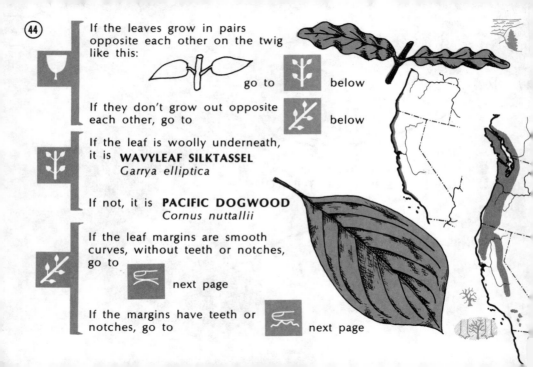

go to below

If they don't grow out opposite each other, go to below

If the leaf is woolly underneath, it is **WAVYLEAF SILKTASSEL**
Garrya elliptica

If not, it is **PACIFIC DOGWOOD**
Cornus nuttallii

If the leaf margins are smooth curves, without teeth or notches, go to next page

If the margins have teeth or notches, go to next page

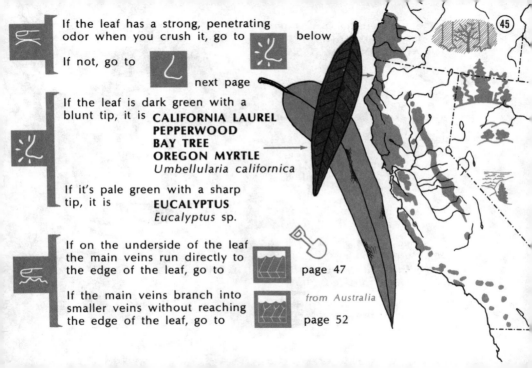

If the leaf has a strong, penetrating odor when you crush it, go to below

If not, go to next page

If the leaf is dark green with a blunt tip, it is **CALIFORNIA LAUREL**
PEPPERWOOD
BAY TREE
OREGON MYRTLE
Umbellularia californica

If it's pale green with a sharp tip, it is **EUCALYPTUS**
Eucalyptus sp.

If on the underside of the leaf the main veins run directly to the edge of the leaf, go to page 47

If the main veins branch into smaller veins without reaching the edge of the leaf, go to page 52

from Australia

45

(46)

If there is conspicuous, smooth, red-brown bark on the branches, it is MADRONE (see p. 57)

If not, go to below

If the undersides of the leaves are golden-yellow, it is
GOLDEN CHINQUAPIN
Castanopsis chrysophylla

If they're not yellow, go to below

If the leaves are about an inch long, with margins rolled under, it is **CURLLEAF MOUNTAIN MAHOGANY**
Cercocarpus ledifolius

If they're longer, go to page 52

If the leaf blades are shorter than two inches, go to below

If they're longer, go to next page

If the leaves are oval with curved veins, it is **PACIFIC SERVICEBERRY** *Amelanchier florida*

If they're not oval, and the veins are straighter, go to below

If the leaf has a wedge-shaped base and a velvety underside, it is

BIRCHLEAF MOUNTAIN MAHOGANY *Cercocarpus betuloides*

If the leaf base is rounded, it is

WATER BIRCH *Betula occidentalis*

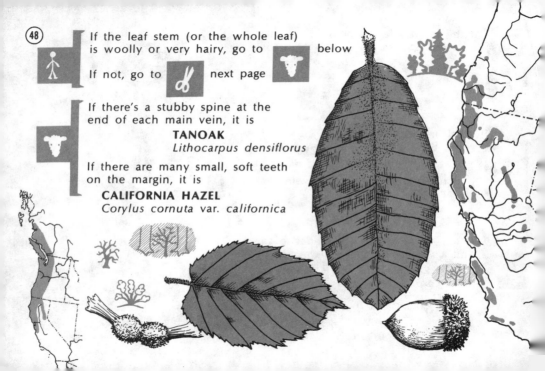

(48)

If the leaf stem (or the whole leaf) is woolly or very hairy, go to below

If not, go to next page

If there's a stubby spine at the end of each main vein, it is

TANOAK
Lithocarpus densiflorus

If there are many small, soft teeth on the margin, it is

CALIFORNIA HAZEL
Corylus cornuta var. californica

If the trunk has white bark, it is
PAPER BIRCH
Betula papyrifera

If the bark isn't white, go to  below

If the leaf margin has sharply pointed teeth and V-shaped notches, go to  below

If the teeth or notches are rounded, go to  page 51

If the tree has thorns, it is
BLACK HAWTHORN
Crataegus douglasii

If not, go to  next page

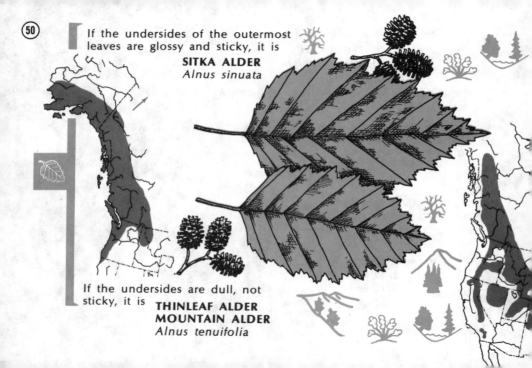

If the undersides of the outermost
leaves are glossy and sticky, it is
SITKA ALDER
Alnus sinuata

If the undersides are dull, not
sticky, it is **THINLEAF ALDER**
MOUNTAIN ALDER
Alnus tenuifolia

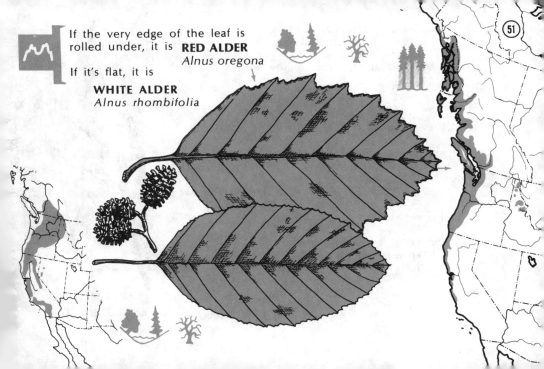

If the very edge of the leaf is rolled under, it is **RED ALDER**
Alnus oregona

If it's flat, it is

WHITE ALDER
Alnus rhombifolia

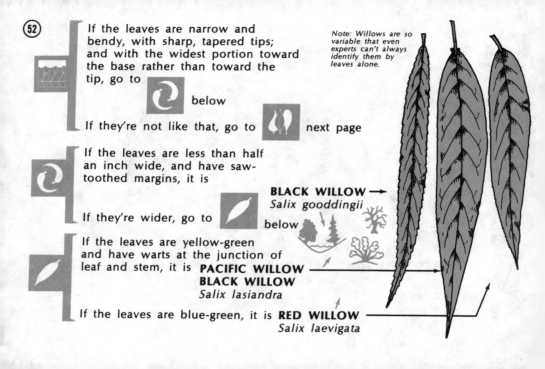

(52)

If the leaves are narrow and bendy, with sharp, tapered tips; and with the widest portion toward the base rather than toward the tip, go to below

If they're not like that, go to next page

Note: Willows are so variable that even experts can't always identify them by leaves alone.

If the leaves are less than half an inch wide, and have saw-toothed margins, it is **BLACK WILLOW** →
Salix gooddingii

If they're wider, go to below

If the leaves are yellow-green and have warts at the junction of leaf and stem, it is **PACIFIC WILLOW**
BLACK WILLOW
Salix lasiandra

If the leaves are blue-green, it is **RED WILLOW** →
Salix laevigata

If the leaves are narrow and paddle-shaped—wider toward the tip, and with a wedge-shaped base like this:

go to below

If they're some other shape, go to page 55

If all leaves have easy-to-see teeth on their margins, go to below

If the teeth are minute or sometimes absent, go to next page

If the leaves are longer than two inches, it is **PACIFIC BAYBERRY WAX MYRTLE** *Myrica californica*

If they're shorter, it is **BITTER CHERRY** *Prunus emarginata*

If the undersides of the leaves are covered with velvety, white hair, it is **SITKA WILLOW SILKY WILLOW** *Salix sitchensis*

If not, go to below

If the leaves have mostly rounded ends and narrowly tapered bases, it is **SCOULER WILLOW** *Salix scouleriana*

If they have more pointed ends, wider bases, and rolled-under margins, it is

ARROYO WILLOW *Salix lasiolepis*

If the leaves have more than 25 teeth along their margins, go to below

If there are fewer teeth or none at all, it's an **OAK.** Go to page 58

If the leaf margin is scalloped with stiff, almost spiny teeth, go to below

If the teeth feel soft, and point toward the leaf tip, go to next page

If the leaf blade is wider toward the base, it is **HOLLYLEAF CHERRY ISLAY** *Prunus ilicifolia*

If it's widest in the middle, it is **CHRISTMASBERRY TOYON** *Heteromeles arbutifolia*

If the leaf tips are pointed like this:

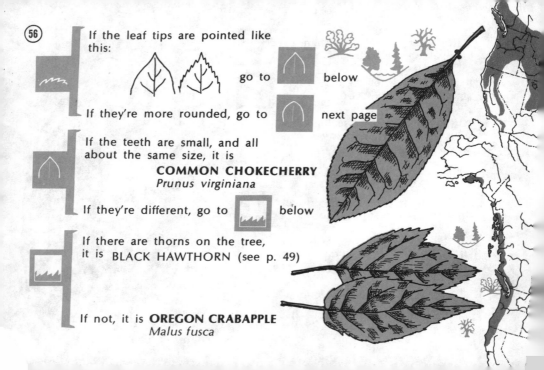

go to below

If they're more rounded, go to next page

If the teeth are small, and all about the same size, it is
COMMON CHOKECHERRY
Prunus virginiana

If they're different, go to below

If there are thorns on the tree, it is BLACK HAWTHORN (see p. 49)

If not, it is **OREGON CRABAPPLE**
Malus fusca

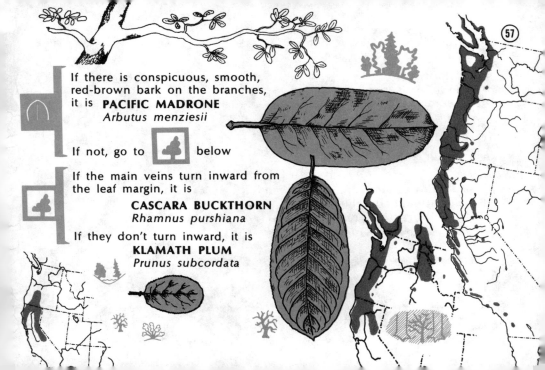

If there is conspicuous, smooth, red-brown bark on the branches, it is **PACIFIC MADRONE**
Arbutus menziesii

If not, go to below

If the main veins turn inward from the leaf margin, it is

CASCARA BUCKTHORN
Rhamnus purshiana

If they don't turn inward, it is

KLAMATH PLUM
Prunus subcordata

58

If the leaves are dark green; or if the bark is blackish, not scaly or checkered, go to **below**

If the leaves are light green or bluish; or if there is scaly or checkered bark, go to **next page**

If the leaves are convex on top and have tufts of hair where the veins join on the undersides, it is **COAST LIVE OAK**
Quercus agrifolia

If the leaves are flatter, hairless, and some are without spines, it is
INTERIOR LIVE OAK
Quercus wislizenii

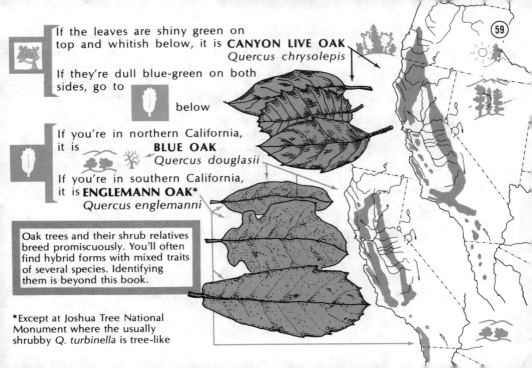

If the leaves are shiny green on top and whitish below, it is **CANYON LIVE OAK**
Quercus chrysolepis

If they're dull blue-green on both sides, go to below

If you're in northern California, it is **BLUE OAK**
Quercus douglasii

If you're in southern California, it is **ENGLEMANN OAK***
Quercus englemanni

Oak trees and their shrub relatives breed promiscuously. You'll often find hybrid forms with mixed traits of several species. Identifying them is beyond this book.

*Except at Joshua Tree National Monument where the usually shrubby *Q. turbinella* is tree-like

INDEX

Other books in the pocket-sized "finder" series:

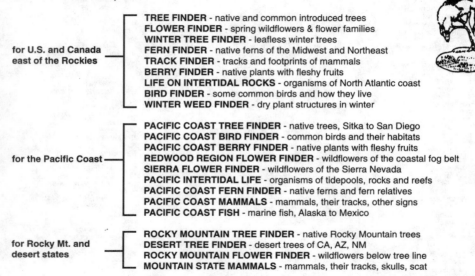

for U.S. and Canada east of the Rockies
- **TREE FINDER** - native and common introduced trees
- **FLOWER FINDER** - spring wildflowers & flower families
- **WINTER TREE FINDER** - leafless winter trees
- **FERN FINDER** - native ferns of the Midwest and Northeast
- **TRACK FINDER** - tracks and footprints of mammals
- **BERRY FINDER** - native plants with fleshy fruits
- **LIFE ON INTERTIDAL ROCKS** - organisms of North Atlantic coast
- **BIRD FINDER** - some common birds and how they live
- **WINTER WEED FINDER** - dry plant structures in winter

for the Pacific Coast
- **PACIFIC COAST TREE FINDER** - native trees, Sitka to San Diego
- **PACIFIC COAST BIRD FINDER** - common birds and their habitats
- **PACIFIC COAST BERRY FINDER** - native plants with fleshy fruits
- **REDWOOD REGION FLOWER FINDER** - wildflowers of the coastal fog belt
- **SIERRA FLOWER FINDER** - wildflowers of the Sierra Nevada
- **PACIFIC INTERTIDAL LIFE** - organisms of tidepools, rocks and reefs
- **PACIFIC COAST FERN FINDER** - native ferns and fern relatives
- **PACIFIC COAST MAMMALS** - mammals, their tracks, other signs
- **PACIFIC COAST FISH** - marine fish, Alaska to Mexico

for Rocky Mt. and desert states
- **ROCKY MOUNTAIN TREE FINDER** - native Rocky Mountain trees
- **DESERT TREE FINDER** - desert trees of CA, AZ, NM
- **ROCKY MOUNTAIN FLOWER FINDER** - wildflowers below tree line
- **MOUNTAIN STATE MAMMALS** - mammals, their tracks, skulls, scat

NATURE STUDY GUILD PUBLISHERS, Box 10489, Rochester, NY 14610, **www.naturestudy.com**